# Part of the Group

# Part of the Group

**Games that Increase
Social Understanding**

Mimi W. Lou, Ph.D.
Elizabeth Stone Charlson, Ph.D.
Stephen M. Gage, M.S., L.P.C.
Nancy Moser, L.C.S.W.

DawnSignPress
San Diego, California

Manufactured in the United States of America
Published by DawnSignPress

The information contained in this book is intended to be educational and not for diagnosis, prescription, or treatment of mental health disorders, whatsoever. This information should not replace competent medical care. The Author and Publisher are in no way liable for any use or misuse of the information.

LIBRARY OF CONGRESS CATALOGING-IN-PUBLICATION DATA

Part of the group : games that increase social understanding / Mimi
   WheiPing Lou ... [et al.]
      p. cm.
   Includes bibliographical references.
   ISBN 1-58121-020-5
   1. Deaf—Education. 2. Deaf children—Education. 3. Social skills—Study
and teaching. 4. Social intelligence—Study and teaching. 5. Educational games.
I. Lou, Mimi WheiPing.

HV2469.S63.P37 2005
371.91'2--dc22                                                2004056202

# Contents

# Introduction

*A* teacher reads a story to her class of middle school deaf/hard
of hearing students. The story has a great moral about drugs
and peer pressure that the teacher wants to get across. After reading the story, she asks the class what they learned from the characters. The students don't respond. She asks how the characters
feel in the story and what influences their decisions. One student
states, "Drugs and alcohol are bad," but no one discusses the
characters. She realizes that she is not getting through to them.

At a job site, a deaf employee arrives to work late and, as usual,
blames others for not getting his work done. The supervisor sits
down with him to talk about the situation. The supervisor tries to
identify the problem by asking the worker how he feels and
what's going on. The worker continues to blame others and is unable to talk about his feelings or how the issue started.

A school counselor initiates a social skills group for deaf high
school students. He uses a role play involving one student throw-
ing a piece of paper at another student and asks the group how
the student being hit with the paper should handle this situation.
Students in the group answer "Wrong to throw paper, mean," but
are unable to talk about how the situation should be handled.
The discussion goes nowhere.

A mental health counselor is facilitating a group with deaf
adults. She initiates a discussion on the topic of friendship and
how to make and keep friends. One group member begins to
complain about her mother. Another group member interrupts and

*begins talking about being bored at home with nothing to do. The counselor struggles to get everyone focused on the same topic.*

Do these situations sound familiar? These scenarios, reported by teachers and counselors, illustrate a problem that is faced by some deaf individuals: difficulties with social skills and understanding social situations. For deaf children and adults, these problems are often related to communication difficulties with others, especially in the family and at school. Communication problems interfere with learning important social concepts such as understanding emotions, seeing a situation from the perspectives of others and having empathy for others, and solving social problems. Poor understanding of social concepts leads to difficulties demonstrating appropriate social behavior and making appropriate decisions. Professionals can help deaf children and adults learn the social knowledge that they are lacking and *Part of the Group* provides one way to do that. This manual uses games and activities to set up "real-life" social situations in which group members can learn important social concepts.

## OVERVIEW

This manual is designed for deaf children, adolescents, and adults and can be used regardless of communication strategy and/or language (e.g., sign, voice, total communication). The manual consists of games that are fun to play and help members acquire important social knowledge. Teachers, counselors, vocational rehabilitation professionals, and independent living counselors can set up and run the games, which are flexible and can be incorporated into most settings. The games focus on learning feeling words, learning about others, communicating better with others, increasing thinking skills about social issues, and improving social problem solving ability. The aim of the program is to help children and adults learn the basic thinking skills that they need to help them build a strong foundation of social knowledge. By increasing social knowledge, participants will be in a better position to display appropriate social behavior. Although the games are designed to help participants learn more about self, others, social events, problem solving, and communication, this is not a didactic program. Social-cognitive learning happens as participants play and have fun and not by lecture from the group facilitator.

## WHAT IS SOCIAL COGNITION?

Social skills and social knowledge are receiving more attention than ever before. Theories such as emotional intelligence or "emotional IQ" are becoming well-known and are helping to spread the message that verbal cognitive ability, mechanical cognitive ability, and math cognitive ability are not all there is to intelligence. There is also social-cognitive ability, which has as much to do with success as other types of intelligence.

So what is social cognition? Social cognition is basically the knowledge and reasoning ability that one has about self, others, social situations, emotions, and social problem solving. This covers a person's ability to identify the emotions of self and others; see a situation from many different perspectives; communicate well with others; understand others, including their personalities, values, likes, and dislikes; and identify problems and think of different solutions for social problems. Psychologists have long believed that a relationship exists between social cognition (knowledge) and social adjustment/social behavior. Stated simply, the more one knows about others, identifying feelings, and solving problems, the better she/he will be able to get along with others, handle conflicts, and deal with her/his feelings in a positive way. People who do not have the knowledge to interact with others appropriately may have problems finding and keeping friends, interacting appropriately with authority figures such as teachers and bosses, and demonstrating appropriate social behavior on the job and/or at school.

The social-cognitive approach used in this manual is helpful with deaf children and adults because it takes a developmental "stepwise" approach. The manual includes a number of games that focus on early developmental steps that help participants build a strong foundation of social learning. The first step covers basic social knowledge, which includes learning feelings words, learning fundamental communication skills, and learning about the feelings, likes and dislikes, and values of others. The next step includes increasing reasoning skills and problem solving skills. From there, participants can take the next steps and begin to learn about how they currently interact with others and how to improve those interactions.

This manual focuses on four different social-cognitive areas that professionals believe are the foundation for appropriate social behavior: communication, person conceptualization, social problem solving, and perspective taking.

- **Communication:** This covers the ability to convey feelings and ideas to another person and also the ability to understand the feelings and ideas that another person is expressing. The games focus on being able to share meaning with other people, rather than on improving language skills per se.

- **Person conceptualization:** This covers how we think about people, in other words, our knowledge about others' personalities, feelings, interests, behaviors, and appearances.

- **Social problem solving:** This includes discussion and negotiation with others in order to work out solutions for a group project or problem.

- **Perspective taking:** This is the ability to view social situations from the perspective of other people or "step into another's shoes."

## SOCIAL COGNITION AND DEAFNESS

Both deaf adults involved with vocational rehabilitation and independent living training and deaf children are reported to exhibit a high rate of social problems. This certainly does not mean that deafness is the problem. In fact, there are deaf children and deaf adults who do not exhibit any problems. Deaf individuals who have deaf parents comprise a group that tends to do well behaviorally and socially. Other groups that do well include deaf children with early positive communication and deaf children with early exposure to manual communication.

Why is the prevalence of social problems higher among certain groups of deaf individuals? One explanation is experiential deprivation. Important people in the deaf child's life, such as family members and teachers, may not communicate well with the child. Not only do some deaf children miss out on direct communication with others, but also they may miss out on the wealth of learning that a language-rich environment, like that of hearing children or deaf children of deaf parents, provides through exposing children to the communication of others. Both of these issues put deaf individuals at risk for gaps and delays in social-cognitive development. Researchers report that deaf children exhibit difficulties understanding how others view situations, processing information correctly, solving problems, communicating, and understanding emotions. Service providers and researchers report that deaf adults receiving vocational rehabilitation and independent living services exhibit difficulties with understanding the perspectives of others and solving problems, and they generally have underdeveloped social skills. Because deaf individuals are at risk for missing out on social learning, professionals should include opportunities for deaf children and adults to acquire basic social knowledge.

## WHY PLAY GAMES?

One of the best ways to learn about social issues is to create real-life situations and provide opportunities for participants to learn by "doing." In contrast to other programs that lecture and instruct about behavior (for example, how to greet another appropriately and appropriate manners at the dinner table), during *Part of the Group* activities participants play games and learn during the process. Many of the activities are common party games that require little preparation from the facilitator. Most of the games require 30 to 45 minutes to complete. However, the time frame for games can vary depending on the size of the group and how much discussion the facilitator generates. In terms of the number of sessions, professionals have used these games for groups as short as 8 weeks and as long as 2 years. The games can be incorporated into a number of settings:

- weekly social skills group time at school;

- during "down" times at school such as during homeroom, before lunch, and at the end of the day;

- in mental health counseling groups;
- with deaf adults receiving independent living services;
- at educational meetings for vocational training;
- in group home settings and meetings with consumers;
- as part of a counseling group on a psychiatric unit.

Using a game format has a number of benefits over teaching the material in a lecture format. First, games have their own natural rewards. Participants work hard and are motivated to learn because they want to do well in the game. There is no need for the facilitator to give tokens or other reinforcers for working hard and giving appropriate responses (that's not real life). Second, the games do not require advanced language or communication skills. Participants learn by doing rather than through discussion and lecture. This helps group participants who have language and communication delays. Third, a game format encourages group members to think of and use more advanced game-playing techniques. Good game-playing techniques require that one understands the other players, their strengths, weaknesses, how to work well with them, and sometimes how to trick them. That's social learning because members are encouraged to think and learn about others. If members are learning how to play the game better then they are improving their social learning at the same time. Fourth, games can be played many times during the course of a group's meeting. Repeating a game encourages group members to use new and more advanced techniques in order to do well. Improving their techniques means that participants are continuing to learn important concepts, even though they are playing the same game. And last, playing games is enjoyable. Often participants do not realize that they are playing an educational game; it's just fun.

## ROLE AND QUALIFICATIONS OF FACILITATOR

Groups can have either one or two facilitators. One facilitator is sufficient for most groups, but participants who need more attention and support, such as psychiatric consumers and groups with elementary-age children, sometimes require two group facilitators. The term "facilitator" is used rather than teacher or leader for good reason: this is not a curriculum to be taught or a set of behavioral lessons that must be directed by a leader. Facilitators support learning, structure learning opportunities, and make learning accessible. Growth occurs as participants play the games and experience the consequences of their actions. If the facilitator is too directive and/or authoritarian, then the real-life and natural consequence feel is lost.

Even though the facilitator is not directing, the facilitator's role is nonetheless active and very important. After setting up the game and providing the materials, the facilitator joins the activity as a regular participant. By joining the game as a participant, the facilitator has the opportunity to model higher-order thinking skills such as problem solving and good game-playing techniques for the other participants. In this way, other participants can learn from the facilitator without the facilitator directly teaching the material. The facilitator has a double role though; not only does he/she participate and act as a role model, but also is active in encouraging participants to think through situations, solve problems, and reflect on what they have learned (for more information about this approach, see mediated intervention developed by Feuerstein under suggested reading).

If the facilitator set up the game and then left to go do paperwork while the participants were playing, how would the participants do? What if one participant didn't communicate as well as the others? Would he/she be left out of the whole game? What if a conflict occurred between two members? Would they drop out of the game? At these critical moments, the facilitator helps each individual use her/his thinking skills to continue participating in the game. That does not mean that the facilitator jumps in and directs the game and tells people what to do, or act like she/he knows the answer or how to solve the problem. The facilitator is involved as an equal participant on the "same level" as the other participants. The facilitator gets involved to help the individuals think through the task, figure out the most effective ways to accomplish the task, reflect on what was learned during the game, praise group members for their thinking skills, and point out issues and approaches that blocked progress in the game.

In terms of qualifications, facilitators who are able to model good game playing for others and support and encourage thinking and learning among participants are good facilitators. Teachers, mental health counselors, group home staff, and vocational rehabilitation counselors have successfully facilitated past groups. The primary responsibilities of facilitators are to (1) plan the activity, (2) make and/or prepare needed materials, (3) participate in the game, (4) encourage group members to do their best and participate in the game, and (5) discuss and review the game with group members. Facilitators do not need formal training in group therapy and/or social cognition because learning happens naturally as group members play the games.

An important consideration for facilitators is that the manual provides the game format, but the facilitator must make each game appropriate for her/his group. This is not a cookbook where everything is laid out. Instead, the games are designed to be a springboard for learning and the facilitator makes the game meaningful for her/his group. This means that facilitators must be knowledgeable about their population. Although special training in group counseling and social cognition is not necessary, facilitators must be able to anticipate which activities and which materials will be appropriate for their group. Facilitators must also adapt their approach depending on the needs of group members. For example, groups with younger children tend to be more animated and move at a slower pace, and the facilitator tends to offer more guidance and positive support than she/he will for groups with deaf adults. With mental health groups, facilitators must choose activities that will not be countertherapeutic for group members. This manual does not provide information about working with various populations and before running a social-cognition group, the facilitator must ask her/himself, "Do I have sufficient knowledge working with this population (e.g., young children, adult vocational rehabilitation consumers, group home residents, mental health consumers) to set up games for them?" The authors recommend that facilitators who do not have experience and training with their specific population either link with a cofacilitator who has such training or seek additional training working with their particular population.

## PAST EVALUATIONS OF *PART OF THE GROUP*

*Part of the Group* was developed at the University of California Center on Deafness (UCCD) in San Francisco as part of a mental health research and training grant from the National Institute of Disability and Rehabilitation Research. The program was developed because professionals in the field of deafness believe that social skills problems interfere with a number of deaf children and deaf adults succeeding in school and at work. Even though many professionals recognize the need for effective social skills training programs, there are no widely accepted social learning programs for deaf adolescents and adults.

Researchers developed the manual and conducted pilot programs with positive results with deaf adults involved in vocational rehabilitation, deaf middle school and high school students in self-contained classrooms, and deaf high school students at a residential school for the deaf. Researchers refined the program, added additional games, and used it with other groups including deaf adults in independent living facilities, deaf adolescents and adults receiving mental health services, and deaf elementary-age children. Since that time, the program has been presented at a number of conferences and disseminated for use by other professionals including staff at residential schools for the deaf, psychiatric facilities, educational programs, and independent living facilities.

## HOW IS THE MANUAL ORGANIZED?
## WHERE DO I START?

The manual is divided into five different sections: (1) Initial Group Session and Warm-Up Activities, (2) Communication Activities, (3) Person Conceptualization, (4) Social Problem Solving, and (5) Perspective Taking. The first section, Initial Group Session and Warm-up Activities, includes directions for the first group session. This initial meeting covers how to explain the program to participants and developing group rules. The first section also includes a list of games (and their page numbers) to use as warm-up activities. These activities are helpful in the beginning stages of a group because (1) they are easy to implement and help the group get off to a good start, (2) they focus on team building and getting to know each other, and (3) these activities give the facilitator a chance to observe the group and get an idea about the skills of the participants to help choose appropriate games in the future. Facilitators should use these warm-up activities for the first three to four meetings of a new group.

Chapters containing the games follow the initial section. The manual is arranged so that activities and games that target a particular learning area are grouped together in the same chapter. The first section focuses on communication, the second section focuses on person conceptualization, the third addresses social problem solving, and the fourth deals with perspective taking. Therefore, if there is a specific learning area that facilitators wish to address, the relevant activities can be easily located. However, facilitators will notice that many activities could fit more than one learning area. For example, some of the perspective taking games also include social problem solving skills. Therefore, facilitators do not need to worry that they must play all the games or that they must jump around to different learning areas each week to make sure that all areas are covered. Because many of the games could fall within a few different learning areas, groups will be exposed to a broad range of social learning no matter what game they play.

Both the chapters and the games in each chapter are sequenced from the least to the most difficult. Communication and person conceptualization are placed early on in the manual (before games related to social problem solving and perspective taking) because developmentally they are generally easier skills to develop. Also, the games near the beginning of each chapter are generally easier to help facilitators choose an activity at an appropriate skill level for their group. Even though activities are categorized and sequenced, they can be implemented in any order. The manual is not arranged so that facilitators go in order from one chapter to the next or one activity to the next. Keep in mind that the activities are not like the learning objectives of a lesson plan in which group members master one game and then move on to the next. Facilitators can pick activities from any chapter at any time. Also, activities should be repeated throughout the year. Group members learn more and practice new skills when they are able to play the same game two or three times. Often, variations are presented in each game so that the game can be repeated with a minor change to make it different. One of the most important rules when choosing activities is to choose activities that the group members enjoy; group members will learn important social concepts if they are fully participating and having fun.

At the beginning of each section is a brief description of the learning area (i.e., communication, person conceptualization, social problem solving, and perspective taking). Also included is a summary of the stages of development within that learning area. The first step describes behaviors that a participant may demonstrate when she/he is in the early stages of learning. The following steps describe behaviors expected from a group member who is advancing her/his learning in this area. If facilitators would like to read more about these areas of social-cognitive learning, a suggested reading list is included on pages 119–120.

The individual games are outlined in a straightforward format.

**Title**

**Activity summary:** brief summary of the activity

**Activity goal**: how the activity specifically benefits the group members

**Materials:** materials used during the activity

**Directions:** description of how the activity is conducted

**Variations/troubleshooting:** describes different ways in which the game can be played and/or repeated and discusses issues that may be encountered during the activity; also outlines ways to make the game easier for younger or less advanced groups.

**Discussion issues:** questions and issues meant to elicit thinking and participation from group members. These questions may make group members conscious of what happened during the activity. *Facilitators should not strive to address all discussion questions* because that would take away from the "game feeling." Instead, pick and choose among the questions as needed.

Sample group member answers to discussion questions are interspersed and written in italics.

The final section of the manual describes some common group problems and suggestions for handling them.

## SUMMARY

Social skills are related to success at school, home, and work. Children who learn social knowledge and social skills demonstrate appropriate behavior in the classroom, get along better with peers, and are able to solve social conflicts that arise. Adults with appropriate social skills often have meaningful relationships, understand what is expected of them by supervisors and counselors, understand the consequences of their actions, express their feelings appropriately, and can solve problems that come up at work and home. Because some deaf children and adults do not have the opportunity to learn important social concepts, teachers and counselors need to provide opportunities for this type of learning. *Part of the Group* is a great way to help deaf children and adults acquire important social knowledge. The games are fun and are easily incorporated into different settings. Past group participants have increased their knowledge of emotions and how to identify the feelings of self and others, have learned to take the feelings of others into account and to "put themselves in other's shoes," and have learned how to solve social problems better. By learning these basic skills, participants build a strong foundation of social learning that they will use for a lifetime.

*A middle school teacher calls in a counselor to work with his class of deaf and hard of hearing students. The teacher complains that "there is so much teasing and bickering; it's like they can't communicate!" In addition, the teacher reports that "they have a hard time talking about feelings and social situations." The counselor uses a* Part of the Group *activity and brings in eight sealed paper bags. The students are curious and become quiet. They want in on the fun. The counselor gives them the task of guessing what's in each bag without looking. The students begin to work together to accomplish the problem solving task at hand.*

# Initial Group Session & Warm-Up Activities

The initial sessions of educational groups establish the mood for the entire group experience. Group members who feel positive about the initial meetings of a group are likely to have good participation and be in a better position to learn in later sessions. In addition, the initial group sessions allow facilitators to learn more about the functioning levels of participants and adapt the activities accordingly. The initial activities focus on establishing group structure and rules, assisting participants in learning each others names and basic personal information, and helping participants feel comfortable with the group format by using games that are not too difficult.

This manual includes one initial group session and a list of five warm-up games that are especially helpful during the first few group meetings. The activity summary for each game and the page number where the complete game can be found are provided. Facilitators should use these warm-up games during the first three or four sessions of a new group.

It is best for the facilitators to familiarize themselves with all the activities in the manual before beginning a program. Knowledge of the entire program, the variations, and options within activities helps facilitators lead participants in becoming "part of the group."

# Initial Group Session

## ACTIVITY SUMMARY

The facilitator informs group members about group goals and group rules.

## ACTIVITY GOAL

1. To establish guidelines and create structure
2. To establish group rules

## MATERIALS

1. One large poster board for each group member
2. Crayons and markers

## DIRECTIONS

Inform participants that for a period of time (specify how long your group will last), the group members will be coming together to learn more about themselves and others. This will be accomplished through group activities and games. Let the group members know that the facilitator will set up the games each week and also will participate as a regular group member for many of the activities.

Next, focus on group rules. Ask group members why is it important to have rules (e.g., to help members feel safe, to inform participants about expected behavior) and ask what rules they want for their group. The facilitator should limit the rules to a short list of general, age-appropriate rules. If the list of rules is too long, group time may be perceived as rigid and no fun. Rules for children and adolescents may include keeping your hands and feet to yourself, talking one at a time, and forbidding name calling or obscenities. Rules for adults may include arriving on time, maintaining confidentiality, and being respectful to one another.

## PERSONAL POSTER

The facilitator should inform the group members that many of the activities and games will encourage the group (including the facilitator) to divulge interesting issues and facts about themselves such as favorite foods, personality type, feelings, and hobbies. These characteristics will be put on a personal poster. For example, a most desired birthday gift is discussed in one activity and that gift will be written on each group member's personal poster. In another activity, we talk about what animal we are most like, and that animal's name will also be written on the personal posters. Facilitators then ask group members to write their names on their posters, and any time new information is learned about a group member it can be written on his/her personal poster. Throughout the duration of the group, facilitators should encourage participants to review each other's personal posters to help learn about each other and discern themes within each person's poster.

If there is time, play the *Pass the Name* game. This game can be completed in about 15 minutes and helps group members learn each other's names. If group members already know each other, you can still play *Pass the Name,* but use the variation described such as favorite sport or favorite food.

# Good Warm-Up Activities

## PASS THE NAME, Page 22

**Activity summary:** Participants memorize other members' names or "favorite things" and then use this knowledge in a competitive game. The game continues with variations that make the game more challenging.

## NOTICE THE CHANGE, Page 40

**Activity summary:** A group member leaves the room, changes something about his/her appearance, and returns to the room, and others try to identify what was changed.

## WHO'S THE LEADER, Page 42

**Activity summary:** Group members imitate the hand or body movements of a leader and change movements when the leader changes. One chosen person must guess who the leader is by observing the group.

## WHAT'S IN THE BAG, Page 76

**Activity summary:** Participants are given sealed bags with different objects inside. By feeling the bags, participants try to identify the objects. Participants must come to a consensus about what is in each bag.

## WALKING GAME, Page 92

**Activity summary:** One person stands in front of the group and depicts an emotion through walking. Others must guess how the person feels and make guesses about why she/he feels that way.

# Communication
# Activities

Communication in this program refers to the ability to share meaning with another. Rather than focusing on vocabulary building and learning rules of language, the games provide opportunities for group members to develop better self-expression and understanding of others. The communication activities in this manual are designed to help members progress through the following steps.

# Communication Steps

**1** Demonstrates understanding of basic interpersonal communication. Uses simple sentences. Attends to others who are talking. Recognizes the relevance of communication. Is able to communicate wants and needs at a basic level.

**2** Asks for clarification some of the time. Is pertinent and logical some of the time. Engages in turn taking. Gives feedback to indicate understanding, such as a head nod. Explains clearly some of the time. Uses simple sentences. Has difficulty with use of facial expression and other nonmanual markers. Has difficulty with activities that rely on discourse with others such as *The Picnic.*

**3** Demonstrates understanding of pragmatics of communication. Changes expressive language to meet the needs of others and the situation a lot of the time. Structures communication to meet the needs of listener and/or situation. Uses adequate range of vocabulary and sentence structure. Explains clearly most of the time. Is comfortable with the games that rely on discourse such as *What's in the Bag* and *The Interview.* Asks questions to understand a lot of the time.

**4** Changes language to meet the needs of others and the situation almost always. Recognizes when others are misunderstanding each other and has the ability to step in and assist in communication. Is pertinent, logical, and clear almost always. Most of the time asks questions if does not understand.

# Pass the Name

## ACTIVITY SUMMARY

Participants memorize other members' names or "favorite things" and then use this knowledge in a competitive game. The game continues with variations that make the game more challenging.

## ACTIVITY GOALS

1. To learn more about each other including names and favorite things
2. To learn about important aspects of communication

## MATERIALS

None

## DIRECTIONS

Group members sit in a circle. The first person says his/her name. The second person says the first person's name and then adds his/her own name. The third person says the first person's name, the second person's name, and then his/her own name, and so on until all group members have participated. If there is a mistake, the process starts over. If group members know each other well prior to this activity, using names to play the game may be boring. Instead, the facilitator may start with a version described under "Variations/Troubleshooting" below, such as using favorite food or favorite sport.

The second round is slightly different. One member says his/her name and then picks another person in the group and says his/her name. The other person must then say his/her own name and then choose another person in the group and say his/her name. If a member misses when his/her name was called, she/he must leave the group. The game continues until most members are out. Members will almost invariably attempt to make the game harder, and this is encouraged. A group member demonstrates higher levels of perspective taking and person conceptualization when they are able to make the activity harder for others. In other words, group members must think about their competitors skills and weaknesses in order to find ways to "trick" them. The group facilitator can model this behavior if group members do not do it on their own by signing/voicing very fast, saying one person's name while looking at a different person, or waiting a long period before responding so that others are not prepared.

## VARIATIONS

1. Substitute favorites such as sports, animals, and foods for names. Write each person's favorite object on his/her personal poster.

## DISCUSSION ISSUES

1. What was the easiest?

   *Our names, because we already know each other's names. What made the game harder? Looking at one person and signing a totally different person's name. Why? Because in communication it is important to look at the person with whom you are talking and sign/voice clearly.*

2. What did you learn about another person?

   *I did not know that John's favorite sport was roller-skating. I thought it was basketball.*

# The Rumor Game

## ACTIVITY SUMMARY

This activity is similar to the popular Telephone Game, during which players pass along a whispered message from person to person to see how the message is altered by the time it reaches the last participant.

## ACTIVITY GOALS

1. To focus on important aspects of clear communication
2. To observe how misunderstandings occur
3. To improve communication with others

## MATERIALS

Videotape equipment is optional.

## DIRECTIONS

Participants stand in a line, all facing forward. The person at the rear of the line is responsible for creating a sentence or story that will be passed down the line. For the first round, the facilitator should take this role and create a sentence tailored to the functioning level of participants. For younger and less advanced groups, use a simple sentence such as, "It is raining and cold outside." For more advanced groups, use a couple of sentences such as, "A boy walked to the store to buy milk; however, the store was out of milk so he bought orange juice instead." The person who creates the sentence/story should write it down so it can be compared to later versions. The person who created the message then taps the back of the person immediately in front. When that person turns, the first participant passes the message. The second participant then turns and repeats the sentence/story to the next in line, repeating it exactly as she/he remembers seeing/hearing it. The message is passed down the line in this manner until it reaches the last person, who then repeats it to the whole group.

Discuss the results, comparing the final sentence with the original sentence. If the group is videotaped, members can watch the videotape to see how the message changed from one person to the next. The game is repeated with a different person starting the message. The message may vary in length from a few words to a full story. If the message changed, ask participants to problem solve on methods for keeping the message consistent (e.g., use a shorter sentence or one word, keep the message concrete, use a topic familiar to all participants). Play the game again, incorporating the techniques for improving communication, and see how well the techniques work.

## VARIATIONS/TROUBLESHOOTING

1. For younger group members, try starting with a one-word message and gradually build up to longer sentences. Facial expressions can also be used. For example, the first person makes a mad facial expression and that facial expression is sent down the line. Younger members may need coaching to help pass the message. The facilitator can stand with each younger group member who is passing the message and help them practice good communication strategies such as looking at each other, asking to repeat the message, and so on.

2. Compare the original mode of communication or language of the message with the final message. Did it change from ASL to signed English or vice versa?

3. Focus one round on retaining the message, verbatim, exactly as it was signed and the next round on retaining the full meaning of the message with less attention paid to its form.

4. Try one round where the game is played "in the open." Participants who have already passed the message are allowed to watch as the message is passed down the line.

5. For participants with lower language skills, ask them to relay certain hand shape and gesture combinations (e.g., cover your eyes and touch your nose).

6. Discourage participants from blaming each other for changes. Instead, focus on how the group as a whole can improve message relay.

7. If lining up is difficult in your classroom, participants can leave the room, two at a time, to pass the message. After the message is passed, one person returns to the room while another person goes outside to get the message.

## DISCUSSION ISSUES

1. Was the task easy or hard? What made it so?

   *Sentence length, familiarity of topic, similarity of participants' language styles, repetition, rehearsal.*

2. What can you do to prevent miscommunication (both in the game and as applied to other environments)?

   *Discuss communication styles, adapting styles, or asking for clarification of unfamiliar words.*

# Act As If

## ACTIVITY SUMMARY

Students use motion and expression to act in a way which depicts accurately a another student's spoken sentence.

## ACTIVITY GOAL

1. To focus on listening skills and following directions

## MATERIALS

1. Make cards with one descriptive sentence written on each. Example (basic—or younger and/or less advanced group members):

   • A bird flying around the room
   • A cow eating grass
   • A worm crawling under a log
   • A boy flying a kite
   • A girl opening her birthday present

   Example (complex):

   • A woman who is sad because she dropped her glass of water and the glass broke
   • A bird catching three worms and feeding them to three baby birds back in the nest
   • A child who is disappointed that she is not included in the basketball game and goes and asks other students if they want to get a separate basketball game started so that she can play

## DIRECTIONS

The facilitator should choose descriptions that are at an appropriate level for the group. For younger group members the facilitator chooses a statement and gives it to one group member (and reads it for them if needed) and that person must act as if he/she is the character in the situation and portray each aspect of the situation. The facilitator judges whether the situation is portrayed accurately. If not, help the child portray the situation correctly. Each group member gets a turn. For older group members divide the group into two teams. One member chooses a card and acts out the statement for her/his team. If the team guesses correctly, they get a point. Encourage team members to communicate and decide on the guess together.

## DISCUSSION

1. What makes this game harder?

   *Longer sentences with more descriptions.*

2. What would make each person's acting clearer?

# Copy My Design

## ACTIVITY SUMMARY

Group members work in teams of two. One team member makes a design out of various objects and then describes the design to another group member who tries to make the same design based on his/her team member's description.

## ACTIVITY GOALS

1. To improve communication skills related to attending to others and following directions
2. To emphasize the importance of understanding the communication style of others during interactions

## MATERIALS

1. One piece of large poster board for each team
2. Items with which team members can make a design. individually wrapped chocolate squares and hard candy work well (participants can eat them when done!), but nonedible items such as coins, marbles, and stones can also be used
3. Chairs for each team

## DIRECTIONS

Divide the group into teams of two and have team members sit on the floor facing each other. Give each team member an equal number of items (chocolates, coins, etc.). More advanced group members may be given 15 to 25 objects each and younger/less advanced group members may be given 5 to 15 objects each. Team members sit on the floor on either side of the chair. The poster board is put between the team members (propped up by the chair) so that the other team member cannot see the design. One team member makes a design such as a square or star on the floor in front of him/her using the items given. The team member who made the design then describes it to his/her team member, who tries to make the same design (with the same number of objects). The team member receiving the instructions cannot ask any questions. The team(s) that have a closely matched design win. Next, have the partners switch roles, but this time the person receiving instructions can ask questions and give feedback.

## VARIATIONS/TROUBLESHOOTING

1. For younger group members, use only a few objects and allow them to ask questions back and forth.
2. This game can be made more difficult by giving teams a mixture of objects (e.g., hard candy and coins) with which to make designs.

## DISCUSSION ISSUES

1. How well did teams do when you couldn't give feedback or ask questions? How important was listening and paying attention? Who had trouble with this? Why?
2. How well did teams do when questions could be asked and feedback given? Was this easier? Why?
3. Who was good at giving directions? Why?
4. Who was good at receiving directions? Why?
5. What type of communication was most effective for this activity (gesture, ASL, English)? Why?

# Interview

## ACTIVITY SUMMARY

Group members are divided into pairs. Pairs take turns questioning each other about their families, growing up, and school. Group members then return to the larger group and report the information obtained from their partner.

## ACTIVITY GOALS

1. To focus on ways of learning about others
2. To improve communication skills related to asking and answering questions

## MATERIALS

None

## DIRECTIONS

Members are told that they will get the opportunity to interview another person and then report their findings back to the group. Members are then paired up and asked to interview their partner using the following questions:

1. Where were you born?
2. Who is in your family?
3. (If signing) When and where did you learn to sign?
4. What do you like to do outside of school/work?

Interviews will take about 10 minutes. After reconvening in the larger group, each person reports on the information obtained from their partner during the interview. After each interviewer has presented the information, ask the interviewee to give feedback on the correctness of the information. If the information was not correct, ask the pair to work together to correct the information. Write the information obtained about each person on his/her personal poster.

## VARIATIONS/TROUBLESHOOTING

1. It might be beneficial to pair up a group member who has difficulties in communication with a member who is a skilled communicator.

2. Use this activity a few times during the group meetings using different and more advanced questions such as, "What do you like to do during your free time?" "What do you see yourself doing five years from now?" "What is your favorite game we have played so far?" For a different challenge, ask the group as a whole to develop their own list of interview questions.

## DISCUSSION ISSUES

1. What is the purpose of the interview?

   *To learn more about others. Maybe we have things in common and would enjoy doing them together.*

2. What other questions would you have liked to ask your partner?

3. Did you like this activity? Why or why not?

4. Did you have trouble understanding your partner or remembering the information?

5. What could you do to improve the communication with your partner?

# Simon Says

## ACTIVITY SUMMARY

The leader (Simon) gives signed or spoken directions to group members. Group members must attend carefully because if the leader does not start his instruction with "Simon says," then the group members do not follow her/his direction.

## ACTIVITY GOALS

1. To improve listening and attention skills
2. To focus on giving and following clear directions

## MATERIALS

None

## DIRECTIONS

The facilitator starts out in the role of Simon and asks group members to stand in a line. The facilitator informs group members that she/he will give them directions like "walk forward" and "turn left." However, they are to follow the directions only if Simon begins the instruction with "Simon says" (e.g., "Simon says walk forward", "Simon says turn left"). If the facilitator says "walk forward," whoever walks forward must leave the game and wait until the next round because "Simon says" was omitted. Simon tries to trick the players into making errors. As participants make errors, the number of players will shrink; whoever is left standing wins the game. After the group members get the hang of the game, the facilitator can ask group members to take turns being Simon.

## VARIATIONS/TROUBLESHOOTING

1. When group members play the Simon role, encourage them

to develop strategies to trick the other players; this helps develop more advanced thinking skills. For example, Simon might tell them to walk to the right, but Simon looks and walks left, thus encouraging players to follow her/him in the wrong way.

2. Some players may consistently be the first one out. For example, children and adults with attention problems have a hard time with this game. In this case, the facilitator can stand beside group members who are consistently having difficulty and assist them in staying in the game by giving helpful cues.

## DISCUSSION ISSUES

1. What techniques did Simon use to trick the group?

2. Was Simon clear with his directions? How could his directions have been clearer (for example, if he said, "go to the door" does he mean the back door or front door?)? What happened when his directions were not clear?

*People were confused and all went different directions.*

# What Am I

## ACTIVITY SUMMARY

Each group member has a piece of paper with the name of a person/object written on it taped onto his/her back. The first person to guess what is written on his/her piece of paper by asking yes/no questions wins.

## ACTIVITY GOALS

1. To help identify the salient characteristics of a person or object
2. To focus on asking and answering questions

## MATERIALS

1. Paper
2. Tape
3. Marker

## DIRECTIONS

The facilitator prepares for the activity by writing names of either objects or people on small pieces of paper that will be taped to participants' backs. For more advanced groups/participants, people well known to the group members can be written on the paper, such as school faculty, group home staff, and movie or music stars. For younger or less advanced participants/groups, use a simpler version, such as objects found in your meeting room. Also, as a group, generate a list of questions that members can use, such as, "Is it big?", "Is it blue?", and "Is it on the floor right now?", and write this on the board for reference during the game.

Each participant gets a piece of paper taped to his/her back and is told to figure out what is on it by asking only yes/no questions to the other group members. The group leader may ask participants to limit their questions to three per person, which will encourage them to communicate with more group members. The first person to figure out who or what is on his/her paper wins. Allow other group members to continue the activity even after there is a winner until all have finished.

## VARIATION/TROUBLESHOOTING

Replay this activity throughout the year, increasing the difficulty each time. For groups that guessed objects initially, have them guess famous people. Also, for advanced groups, when guessing people, have them focus on one category of questions. For example, when using the category of teachers in our school or other group members, all questions must deal with personality (e.g., Is this person quiet? Is this person hot tempered? Is this person energetic? Is this person aloof? Is this person shy?). Facilitators may need to write down a few examples of personality questions on the board to help group members.

## DISCUSSION ISSUES

1. Which questions helped you the most in guessing your person/object? Why?
2. Which questions were the hardest for others to answer?

# Person
# Conceptualization

P erson conceptualization refers to the sophistication level of a person's understanding of self and others. It covers what we notice about others and how well we know others, including one's physical characteristics, personality characteristics, and traits. When asked to describe others, individuals who function at lower levels of person conceptualization tend to focus on objective information, such as physical characteristics alone. In contrast, individuals who function at higher levels of person conceptualization not only describe others in terms of physical characteristics, but also add personality information and traits and may even provide explanations for how a person's personality developed.

The steps here, based on the descriptive work of Peevers and Secord (1973) and Livesley and Bromley (1973), can be used as a guide for thinking about how person conceptualization develops. The examples at the top are lower level skills, the bottom examples are more sophisticated skills. Please keep in mind that development in this area does not occur rapidly. Raising levels of person conceptualization occurs over a number of years.

# Person Conceptualization Steps

**1** Describes people in terms of objective information; mostly focuses on physical appearance. "He is tall. She has red hair. He is thin."

**2** Describes others in informative ways, but does not use many personality descriptions. Focuses on appearance, behavior, activities, interests, and how that person relates to oneself: "He has red hair. He plays with me. He is my brother."

**3** Describes personality traits, abilities, skills, achievements, beliefs, values: "She likes football. She is polite. She is a hard worker."

**4** Personality traits and dispositions are modified, qualified, specified or elaborated: "He is polite and respectful to all kids in the class, but sometimes rude to adults in the class."

**5** Traits and dispositions are explained psychologically: "He is polite; I think since he has been teased by others, he knows how it feels to be treated badly so he is polite to all."

# Notice the Change

## ACTIVITY SUMMARY

A group member leaves the room, changes something about his/her appearance, and returns to the room, and others try to identify what was changed.

## ACTIVITY GOALS

1. To notice physical aspects of others
2. To learn about the concept of obvious versus subtle change

## MATERIALS

None

## DIRECTIONS

One person is chosen to be first. She/he is asked to stand in front of the group so that members can make a mental picture of her/his appearance. The person then leaves the room and changes some aspect of her/his appearance. For example, the person may roll up sleeves, untie shoes, or take off her/his watch. The person then returns and group members guess what was changed. The first person to correctly guess is then the next person to leave the room and make a change. Group members are encouraged to make subtle changes that others will have a hard time noticing.

## VARIATIONS/TROUBLESHOOTING

Sometimes group members will change things that are not readily visible, such as pulling down socks. Also, when trying to figure out the change, some group members will want to touch the person. During instances like this, the facilitator should continue a nonauthoritarian attitude and instead "facilitate" group thinking and problem solving in regard to these issues. The facilitator might say, "I notice that you chose to change something which we could not see. How does that affect the game? Should we make a rule about this?" and "I noticed that some of you touched one another to figure out what had changed. How do you feel about this? Should we make a no-touching rule?"

## DISCUSSION ISSUES

1. What was easy to guess? Hard to guess? Why?
2. How did you make the game harder?

   *We changed things that were barely visible. Changed something that people don't usually notice.*

# Who's the Leader

## ACTIVITY SUMMARY

Group members imitate the hand or body movements of a leader and change movements when the leader changes. One chosen person must guess "who's the leader" by observing the group.

## ACTIVITY GOALS

1. To focus on group cooperation
2. To encourage problem solving

## MATERIALS

None

## DIRECTIONS

Choose one person to leave the room. The remaining group members pick a leader who will initiate hand or body movements such as hand clapping, head rolling, and so on. Every so often, the leader will change her/his movements, such as changing from hand clapping to jumping up and down. The other group members imitate the leader, copying all movements and changes of movements. The object is for the other participants to follow the leader as closely as possible. The outside person enters the room and stands in the middle of the group. She/he watches group members and attempts to determine who is the leader by noticing clues, such as who is lagging behind and therefore obviously cannot be the leader and who all group members are looking at to get the next movement. She/he gets three guesses. If she/he is correct, she/he enters the group and the leader leaves the room to be the next identified player. If she/he is incorrect, she/he leaves the room, a different leader is chosen, and she/he tries again one more time.

## DISCUSSION ISSUES

1. How did you identify the leader?

   *She/he seemed the most confident in the hand movements. Joe was slightly behind at one point, and Mary was slightly behind the group at another point, so it helped me to narrow it down.*

2. What was your favorite position: guesser, leader, or follower? Why?

3. How did you try to make it hard to guess when you were the leader or when you were the follower?

# The Gift

## ACTIVITY SUMMARY

Group members draw a slip of paper from a container that has the name or picture of a gift on it. They must guess which member in the group wanted that particular gift.

## ACTIVITY GOALS

1. To make inferences about another based on previously learned information about that person
2. To understand others better

## MATERIALS

1. Copies of worksheet titled "The Gift" for each group member (page 46)

## DIRECTIONS

Give each participant a worksheet and ask him/her to write or draw the gift he/she would most want for a birthday present. Ask them not to write their names on the worksheet or to show anyone what they have written or drawn. When all have finished, put the worksheets in a container. Each member then chooses a worksheet from the container and, using the knowledge that they have about the other members, tries to guess who wanted that particular gift. Members take turns telling the group their guesses about who wanted the gift they picked and explaining the reason for making that guess. Discuss whether the guesses are correct. Give the gift worksheet back to the person who made it and ask them to talk about the reasons for wanting that gift. Attach each person's gift worksheet to his/her personal poster.

# VARIATIONS/TROUBLESHOOTING

1. Members often ask how to spell the gift. Also, it may be tempting for the facilitator to correct the spelling of gifts. Because the program tries to avoid seeming academic, the facilitator should not correct spelling errors. If a member asks for help, encouragement can be given to "try your best" or "don't worry about it." For members who have a difficult time writing, pictures can be drawn or cut out of magazines.

2. There can be many variations of this activity, including writing/guessing a favorite food, favorite sport, or favorite TV show. Use this activity at different times during the year with these different topics.

3. It is important for group facilitators to guide participants in evaluating their guesses. Their guesses should be supported by previously learned knowledge (example: I think Karen wants the cat for her birthday because she has a bird, two fish, and a dog at home). It is beneficial for the facilitator to support inferences made about group members based on facts gathered (example: I guess Karen really likes animals). It is also beneficial for group members to get feedback on how they are viewed by others and to understand this different perspective (example: Karen says, "Nope, I don't want a cat for my birthday. In fact, the animals at home are my brother's. I hate animals, but I can see why you thought that I would like them.").

# DISCUSSION ISSUES

1. Why did you choose that person? What do you know about that person that helped you make your guess?

2. Why did the person choose that particular gift?

# GIFT WORKSHEET

# Learn About
# Us Bingo

## ACTIVITY SUMMARY

Individuals answer questions written on a bingo card regarding other group members.

## ACTIVITY GOALS

1. To encourage learning about others
2. To improve communication skills around asking and answering questions

## MATERIALS

1. Facilitators will need to prepare bingo cards prior to the actual game and part of this preparation will need to be done during an actual group session. First, group members must complete a questionnaire (p. 49) and this information will be used to prepare the bingo card (p. 50). Make a copy of the bingo questionnaire for each group member, and in a session prior to the actual bingo game ask them to complete the questions (some group members may need assistance reading the questions and writing their answers). This takes about 10 minutes to complete. Facilitators then use this information to complete the bingo card. After all group members have completed the questionnaire, randomly choose answers from the group members' questionnaires to fill in the bingo card. Do not write the group member's name on the bingo grid; just write down the questionnaire answer or "fact" about the member in the grid. The result will be one bingo card with different facts about the group members on it. Make a copy of this bingo card for each group member.

2. Pencils

# DIRECTIONS

Distribute prepared bingo cards to all group members. Inform the group members that the card includes information or facts about group members. The goal is to correctly identify the group member who fits each box on the card. For example, the first box, "born in," might have "Texas" written down and you try to identify who was born in Texas; write that person's name in that box. The second box, favorite color, might have "orange" written down and you try to identify the group member whose favorite color is orange and write her/his name in that box. If you do not know who fits each description then you will need to ask your group members and figure out who fits each one. The first person to fill in all squares wins the game; however, all participants should be encouraged to complete the activity.

# VARIATIONS/TROUBLESHOOTING

1. Facilitators can repeat this activity with the same bingo card questions, but use different information from the group members' questionnaires.

2. Facilitators can design their own bingo cards with questions that are more personalized and/or advanced such as, "Who told the group during the first session that they are easily embarrassed?" and/or "Who gets mad when others tease him/her?"

# DISCUSSION ISSUES

1. How many questions did you know the answer to and on how many did you have to ask others?

2. What new information did you learn about someone?

3. Are there other questions you would like on the bingo card?

# Bingo Questionnaire

## ABOUT ME

1. I was born in _____

2. My favorite hobby is/what I like to do _____

3. My birthday _____

4. Number of people in my family _____

5. My favorite movie _____

6. My favorite animal _____

7. I am _____ years old

8. My favorite class in school is _____

9. When I grow up I want to be (job) _____

10. Number of pets I have at home _____

11. My favorite present is _____

12. I love _____

# Basic Bingo Card

| | | |
|---|---|---|
| I love | Hobby | Born in |
| Favorite movie | Number of family members | Birthday |
| Favorite present | Favorite school subject | Favorite animal |
| How many pets I have | Job I want | Years old |

# Picture Descriptions

## ACTIVITY SUMMARY

Teams compete to see which can list the most descriptions of a picture.

## ACTIVITY GOALS

1. To improve understanding of others through differentiating among physical, personality, and emotional characteristics

## MATERIALS

1. Pictures of people (from magazines, books, posters, etc.); it is helpful to choose a wide range of pictures that will show people from various ethnic groups, with various physical characteristics, and expressing various feelings

## DIRECTIONS

Depending on the level of the group, the facilitator may wish to review feelings (p. 98) and personality characteristics (p. 55). Personality characteristics and feelings can be written on the board for reference during the activity. After review, the group leader shows one picture of a person to the group. The leader makes three categories on the board: feelings, personality characteristics, and physical characteristics (omitting personality characteristics for younger and less advanced groups as needed). As a group, members first identify this person's feelings. These are listed on the board. For example, for a person sitting on a mountain smiling, the group may list the words relaxed, happy, satisfied, hopeful, fulfilled. Next, members make a list of personality characteristics such as ambitious and goal oriented, hard worker, and dedicated if the pictured person climbed the mountain. Finally, group members work on physical characteristics such as tall, brown hair, blue eyes, and so on. When all group members seem to understand the activity, they are then divided into teams (maximum of three people to each team). One picture is then posted for all teams to use and teams generate lists of characteristics for all three categories. Each team tries to come up with as many descriptive words as they can within a 5-minute time period. Teams must justify their descriptions and all participants vote on any disputed ones. The team with the most descriptions is considered the winner.

## VARIATIONS/TROUBLESHOOTING

1. Some groups may have a difficult time differentiating among feelings, personality, and physical characteristics. If so, it may help to draw the outline of a person on the board and talk about feelings being on the inside of the person and physical characteristics being on the outside. Personality can be listed below this person and described as "his/her tendency," "his/her way," or what this person is like. It is common for groups to have an easier time working with physical characteristics than personality characteristics.

2. For a more difficult task, divide physical characteristics into "things that can be changed" and "things that can't be changed." This encourages group members to evaluate physical characteristics in a more in-depth way.

3. For a variation, instead of using pictures, use members from the group. Ask someone to volunteer to stand in front of the class and have teams describe them following the directions above. Many students, especially ones who tend to act out, are more cooperative when they are being described. If needed, establish a game rule saying that there can be no negative comments about the person being described.

## DISCUSSION ISSUES

1. What clues do you have as to how the person in the picture feels? What about her/his personality characteristics?

2. Which category is the hardest to complete? Is it harder to list personality or physical characteristics? Why?

# Need a Job

## ACTIVITY SUMMARY

Teams compete to see which can come up with the most qualifications and personality characteristics for a given job. Then a vote is taken to see which group members would be appropriate for that job. (This game is probably not a good game for younger members or lower functioning members.)

## ACTIVITY GOALS

1. To focus on the ways that personality characteristics influences one's job choices

2. To encourage students to think about other group members' personalities in a problem solving game

## MATERIALS

1. Make cards with names of professions on them (e.g., counselor, stock clerk, airplane pilot, teacher, interpreter, park ranger, office manager, nurse, doctor, secretary, mechanic). Make sure to choose professions with which participants are familiar.

2. If needed, a list of sample personality characteristics can be visible during the game (see page 55 for sample personality characteristics).

## DIRECTIONS

Divide group members into teams of two or three. As a review, choose a card with a profession printed on it and all teams work on this one profession. The goal is for teams to brainstorm as many job qualifications and personality characteristics as they can for this job. Discuss qualifications for jobs and generate examples of job qualifications with the whole group to review this concept. For example, if the job of teacher is used, qualifications and characteristics may include college degree, patient, good with children, able to communicate well with parents, and good writing skills. Another card is chosen and teams then work on developing personality characteristics and qualifications for this job. When finished, they present the qualifications and personality characteristics that they have developed and the group decides whether the characteristics are appropriate. If there is disagreement, group members can vote on the item. Majority rules. After the judging, the team with the longest list of accurate qualifications and personality characteristics wins. The group as a whole can discuss who in the group has the characteristics which fit the job. Write this information on that person's personal poster.

## DISCUSSION ISSUES

1. For what jobs was it easy to come up with personality characteristics? For what jobs was it hard? Why?

2. Why do you think that a specific group member would do well in that particular job?

# Personality
# Characteristics

| | |
|---|---|
| Confident | Loyal |
| Strong willed | Sympathetic |
| Controlling | Tolerant |
| Orderly | Inquisitive |
| Reserved | Quiet |
| Shy | Perfectionistic |
| Sensitive | Competitive |
| Friendly | Practical |
| Optimistic | Detailed |
| Energetic | Predictable |
| Fun-loving | Loving |
| Spontaneous | Selfish |
| Sensitive | Mean |
| Calm | Nice |
| Warm | Helpful |
| Thoughtful | Dislikes change |
| Patient | Enjoys change |
| Good listener | Enjoys popularity |

# The Horoscope

## ACTIVITY SUMMARY

Through a group activity, personality descriptors are matched to participants. Participants compare the descriptors that were matched to them with their actual Chinese zodiac signs.

## ACTIVITY GOALS

1. To focus on better understanding others and how one is perceived by others
2. To learn about the characteristics of one's personality

## MATERIALS

1. Identify the Chinese zodiac sign of each group member. Make a photocopy of each person's sign, including the personality descriptions below each sign. Cut out each individual description and put all of these into a container.

2. Make a second copy of Chinese zodiac signs along with the personality descriptions for each group member from the manual and save for later. These do not need to be cut up.

3. Provide a piece of construction paper for each group member on which to attach personality descriptions that the group members acquire.

## DIRECTIONS

Inform group members that a game will be played with Chinese zodiac signs. Give a short explanation about the zodiac (twelve astrological signs in the form of animals, each having its own personality characteristics ascribed to it; people are said to have the personality characteristics of their astrological sign). Tell group members that they each will be given zodiac-based personality descriptions by other group members and that these will be compared with their actual zodiac sign later. Each group member then takes turns choosing a personality description from the container and decides whom it best describes and gives it to that person. The game continues in this manner until all zodiac descriptions have been assigned. Each member is then given their printed zodiac sign (copied earlier). Group members compare what was assigned to them by the other group members to their actual zodiac sign. These descriptions are attached to each person's personal poster.

## VARIATIONS/TROUBLESHOOTING

1. Facilitators may want to give veto power to the person being assigned a personality description to safeguard against hurt feelings. For example, Sally chooses "stubborn" from the container and assigns it to John. John disagrees and feels angry and hurt. A rule already in place giving veto power to John would allow him to get feedback on how he is seen by others, but at the same time he could reject the description and not be stuck with it. Veto power may be appropriate for groups at early stages of getting to know each other, at stages of building trust, or for younger groups.

2. The activity can be modified for more advanced groups. Ask each member to fold his/her piece of construction paper. On the outside, attach the characteristics that are received, but are not really how one feels inside (i.e., this is how I'm seen by others, but not how I really am). On the inside, attach characteristics that are both how one perceives oneself and how others perceive him/her (i.e., this is how I'm seen by others and I agree with it; it is how I see myself also).

3. In that this is not a therapy group, keep the focus on identifying personality characteristics. Avoid in-depth personality exploration. Keep the conversation light.

## DISCUSSION ISSUES

1. Why did you decide to give people a particular description?
2. Do you think the descriptions you received fit you?
3. What do you think about how others see you? Are you surprised?

# Chinese Zodiac

**RAT**    (1936, 1948, 1960, 1972, 1984, 1996)

Ambitious
Honest

Spends money freely
Friendships with many people

**OX**    (1937, 1961, 1973, 1985, 1997)

Bright
Patient

Happy being alone
Outstanding parent

**TIGER**    (1938, 1950, 1962, 1974, 1986, 1998)

Aggressive
Courageous
Inspiring

Candid
Sensitive

**RABBIT**    (1939, 1951, 1963, 1975, 1987, 1999)

Luckiest of all signs
Talented
Articulate

Affectionate
Shy
You speak peace throughout your life

**DRAGON**    (1940, 1952, 1964, 1976, 1988, 2000)

Eccentric
Has a complex life

Passionate nature
Abundant health

**SNAKE**    (1941, 1953, 1965, 1977, 1989)

Wise
Intense
Attractive

Vain
High tempered

## HORSE  (1942, 1954, 1966, 1978, 1990)

Popular                   Often ostentatious
Attractive                Needs people
Impatient

## SHEEP  (1943, 1955, 1967, 1979, 1991)

Elegant                   Timid
Creative                  Prefers anonymity

## MONKEY  (1944, 1956, 1968, 1980, 1992)

Very intelligent          Able to influence people
Enthusiastic achiever     Easily discouraged and confused

## ROOSTER  (1945, 1957, 1969, 1981, 1993)

Pioneer in spirit         Seeks knowledge
Devoted to work           Sometimes selfish and eccentric

## DOG  (1946, 1958, 1970, 1982, 1994)

Loyal                     Works well with others
Honest                    Stubborn
Generous                  Wants many things

## BOAR  (1947, 1959, 1971, 1983, 1995)

Noble                     Makes life-long friends
Chivalrous                Frequent conflicts with friends

# The Lunch Date

## ACTIVITY SUMMARY

Group members identify the type of person that other group members would like for a lunch date. Group members then tell with whom they would actually like a date.

## ACTIVITY GOALS

1. To encourage group members to consider other's perceptions, feelings, and characteristics

## MATERIALS

1. Cut out five pictures of different types of people from magazines (include representatives from different ethnic, age, and disability groups). Number the pictures 1 to 5.
2. Paper and pencil for each group member

## DIRECTIONS

The group members are told that each of them is going out to lunch tomorrow with one of the people in the pictures. The purpose of this lunch date is to get to know an interesting person better, learn more about their profession, and/or ask for his/her opinion. Each member can choose with whom she/he wants a lunch date. Ask the participants to look at each picture and write down the picture number of the person with whom they would like to go to lunch, but do not show the other participants.

Next, ask them to think about their groupmates. Members write down the number of the person whom they think that each groupmate would choose to go out to lunch with. When all have finished, identify one person to be first. Each group member tells with whom they think this person would like to go out on a lunch date. This person then reveals whom they actually picked. The activity proceeds in this manner until all members have been the focus of the discussion. On each person's personal poster, write down whom they choose for a lunch date and who other people picked for them.

## VARIATIONS/TROUBLESHOOTING

For a competitive game, points can be given for correct answers.

## DISCUSSION ISSUES

1. Why do you think the group member wants to go out with that person?
2. Why do you want to go out with that person?
3. Was it easy or hard to guess?
4. What did you learn about each other during this activity?

# Snapshot

## ACTIVITY SUMMARY

Participants take pictures of each other (preferably using an in-stamatic or digital camera), and these pictures are attached to construction paper. Pictures are then passed around the room and members write sentences under each picture that describes the person in the photo.

## ACTIVITY GOALS

1. To increase understanding of others
2. To consider how one is perceived by others

## MATERIALS

1. Camera
2. Construction paper
3. Tape
4. Markers
5. Poster board for each person
6. Color printer (for digital photos)

## DIRECTIONS

Group members are asked to take turns designing a backdrop on posterboard for pictures that will be taken of them. Examples of what members might draw include their names in over-size letters, a self-portrait, graffiti, their school logo, their favorite sports team, or a nature scene. When their backdrop is done, the group member stands in front of her/his creation and another group member takes her/his picture. Each group member proceeds in this manner until all have finished. While creating the backdrops, members should be encouraged to look at other students' work, comparing the preferences for different backdrops.

The pictures are then attached to pieces of construction paper for each member. The pictures are then passed around to the group members. Group members can draw pictures or write sentences on the paper to describe the person in the picture. Encourage members to list personality characteristics and likes and dislikes. Members can look at the personal posters to get assistance and even copy items from the personal posters. For younger group members or less advanced group members, focus on concrete descriptions such as pets at home, number of siblings, and favorite foods instead of personality.

When all have finished, the pieces of construction paper are put facedown in the middle of the group. Group members take turns choosing one person's picture and, without telling the name, read the descriptions written about this person. Group members are instructed to listen to the descriptions and identify which one is theirs. Attach each person's picture to his/her personal poster.

## VARIATIONS/TROUBLESHOOTING

If no camera is available, group members can take turns drawing outlines of each other on poster paper. Descriptions are written on this poster paper.

## DISCUSSION ISSUES

1. What do you think about the descriptions written about you?

2. How did you come up with the descriptions that you assigned to others? Explain why you wrote those.

3. Did the backdrops of the pictures help you think of descriptions?

# Animal Personalities

## ACTIVITY SUMMARY

Group members assign personality characteristics to animals and then vote on which group member is most like each animal.

## ACTIVITY GOAL

1. To focus on the personalities of others

## MATERIALS

1. Pencils and construction paper for each person
2. Various magazines that have pictures of animals in them
3. Container to hold slips of paper

## DIRECTIONS

The facilitator begins the group by reviewing personality words as needed (see personality characteristics, p. 55). These can be written on a blackboard. After review, the facilitator displays an animal picture and the group as a whole assigns personality characteristics to fit this animal. For example, if an old hound dog is chosen, characteristics such as loving, wise, lazy, nice, friendly, looking for affection, and faithful may be appropriate. When all group members seem to understand this activity, the group proceeds to the game aspect.

All group member's names are put into a container. Each member then chooses a name and looks in the magazines for an animal that fits this person. The picture is cut out, paper is glued to the back of it, and personality characteristics are listed which describe both the animal and the person. When all have finished, pictures are presented together with an explanation of how the animal is similar to the particular group member. Attach pictures to each person's personal poster.

## VARIATIONS/TROUBLESHOOTING

Group members are asked not to choose degrading pictures. Group members can have the final judgement on pictures that are assigned to them.

## DISCUSSION ISSUES

1. How did you choose that animal? What are the characteristics that are appropriate for that person?
2. How is that animal *not* like that person?
3. Does everyone agree that that animal is like that person? Do you want to vote?
4. Do you like the animal that was assigned to you?
5. How does the animal that was assigned to you compare with your favorite animal?
6. What animal would you choose for yourself? Why?

# The Collage

## ACTIVITY SUMMARY

Each group member makes a collage that describes her/himself. The collages are then put in a stack, and members take turns choosing a collage and guessing who made it.

## ACTIVITY GOAL

1. To identify unique aspects of oneself

2. To encourage participants to use the information that they have about others when making decisions

## MATERIALS

1. Various magazines

2. Scissors and glue

3. Colored construction paper

## DIRECTIONS

Members choose pictures from magazines that describe themselves and make a collage with these pictures. When all have finished, the collages are put into a stack, and members take turns choosing a collage. They examine the collage and guess who made it. Each member then explains his/her guess to the group. The person who made the collage explains why she/he chose the pictures in the collage. Attach each person's collage to his/her personal poster.

## VARIATIONS/TROUBLESHOOTING

1. Some members may be concrete about choosing pictures. Others may choose symbolic pictures, such as a picture of the sun, to show that they are lively, like a ball of fire. The facilitator may model the use of abstract pictures.

2. Have the group members choose names from a container and make a collage that describes that person.

## DISCUSSION ISSUES

1. How did you guess who made that collage? Why?

2. What did you already know about that person that was represented on the collage?

3. What did you *not* know about that person that is on the collage?

4. Is there an important characteristic about that person that is missing from the collage?

5. Tell us about your collage. How does it describe you?

# Dream House

## ACTIVITY SUMMARY

Group members build their "dream house" out of facilitator-provided materials.

## ACTIVITY GOALS

1. To explore one's values and needs
2. To increase one's understanding of others' personalities, values, and needs

## MATERIALS

1. Materials to build a house: this can be as simple as providing members with paper and pencils to draw their houses or giving them shoe boxes (or other small boxes) and they can cut in windows, draw in the floor plan, and paste on a large sheet of paper that will act as the lawn. Or it can be creative and complex by providing various materials (clay, sticks, paper, candy, etc.) and having members build small houses. Make sure that members have enough materials to add various objects to their houses such as a hot tub or tree house.

## DIRECTIONS

Start off with a brief group discussion about differences in houses (some have swimming pools, some have art rooms and libraries, some are small, some have a big back yard, some have a huge living room, some have a sun room, etc.). Discuss the reasons for differences in homes. People have different needs and values (e.g., a person who loves to cook may want a big kitchen, a person who is athletic may want a swimming pool, a person who values cultural activities may settle for a small house in the city, a person who loves movies may build a personal theater, a person who is easily claustrophobic may want a huge house on a farm in the country, a person who wants a large family may want a big house, etc.). Inform members that everyone in the group today will build a house that fits their wishes. The facilitator may want to give an example of something that she/he will make sure to include in her/his house. As participants are working on their houses, encourage them to think of all the things they need and want in their houses.

After all group members have built a house, they present their houses to the group. Each member makes a list of the needs that his/her house includes and describes these to the group. The activity can either end with each group member presenting her/his house or a winner can be chosen. One option for choosing a winner is to identify the person who built the house with the most characteristics. Another option for choosing a winner is to have group members vote on the most creative house.

## VARIATIONS/TROUBLESHOOTING

For more advanced groups, have each person build a house for another person in the group, making sure to include items in the house that fit the person's values, likes, and dislikes.

## DISCUSSION ISSUES

1. Was there something that you saw on another person's house that you would now like to add to yours?
2. How were all the houses similar? Did you include flashing lights for the doorbell and phone (if deaf/hard of hearing)?

# The Badge

## ACTIVITY SUMMARY

Individuals create badges in the shape of stars for other participants. The stars are labeled with various positive attributes of
the group member and are then presented to that person. This
activity can be repeated throughout the time that the group
meets, but is especially fitting for the last group session because the badges can be "awards" that group members take
with them.

## ACTIVITY GOALS

1. To encourage group members to think about and express
   statements about positive aspects of others
2. To get members' feedback about positive aspects of oneself

## MATERIALS

1. Copy enough of the badges (p. 72) so that each participant
   can make a badge for each member of the group.
2. Implements for writing and drawing on the badges including colored pencils, pens, and crayons
3. Scissors
4. Ribbons, glue, sparkles, and stickers to decorate badges
   (optional)

## DIRECTIONS

Give each participant enough badges to make one for each
group member. Ask participants to think of characteristics that
they like about each member of the group and write/draw
those attributes on the badges. Facilitators should emphasize
that only positive attributes can be used. Facilitators can en-

courage members to look at the personal posters to get an idea of what to include on the badge. Each member then explains the badges that she/he made and then gives them to the intended recipients. Attach each person's badges to his/her personal poster.

## VARIATIONS/TROUBLESHOOTING

1. Put all completed badges in a container and ask group members to choose a badge and guess for whom it was designed.

2. If members have a difficult time writing on the badges, drawings can be used. The group goal is for participants to think about what they like about another person and be able to express it to that person.

## DISCUSSION ISSUES

1. How many of your badges were similar?

2. Do you agree with the badges you were given?

3. Which badge did you like the best? Which badge was the most surprising? How do you feel about your different badges?

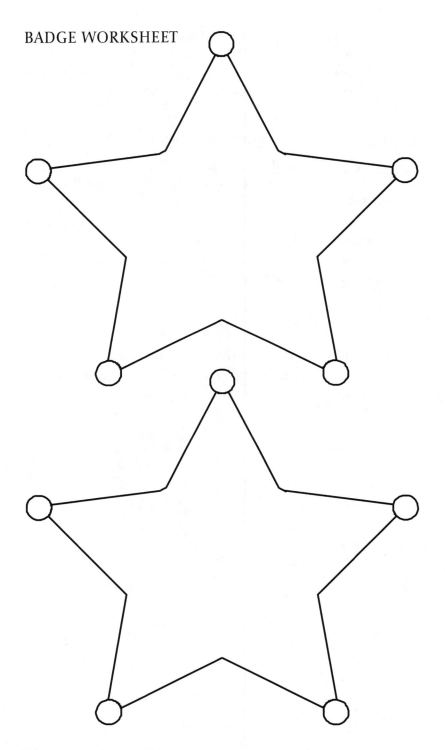

# Social Problem Solving

Most people view problem solving as thinking of many solutions to a problem and evaluating the consequences of each choice. The choices are not viewed as "correct" or "incorrect"; there are different desirable choices depending on the situation. In contrast, social problem solving activities in this manual tend to have a well-defined goal (i.e. correct outcome); if group members do not plan or work well together, then they experience a negative consequence. The negative outcomes are then discussed and linked back to the group process. For example, during a picnic planning exercise, if the group does not plan for the picnic appropriately they could end up lacking items that they need for the picnic, such as utensils or drinks. The steps here can be used as a guide for thinking about how social problem solving develops. The description at the top is consistent with lower level skills and the bottom examples describe more sophisticated behaviors.

# Social Problem Solving Steps

1    Takes action regarding a problem without discussing with others. Does not collaborate. Does not seek the opinions of others, or is passive; lets others solve the problem. Does not see the consequences of her/his actions.

2    Is involved with others, but not collaboratively. Works side by side, but not with others. Does not exchange ideas. Either tells others what to do or follows the directions of others.

3    Talks and plans with others. Responds to the ideas of others. Introduces ideas to discuss before taking action. Works with others to modify the plan throughout the activity. Engages in conversation about consequences of choices.

4    Collaborates with others. Is able to step outside of the situation and view task as a whole before taking action. Takes into account the strengths and weaknesses of others while planning; creates solutions that integrate the needs of both self and others. Generates a few alternatives to the task/problem and realizes the consequences of each. Helps others get involved in the group problem solving task.

# What's in the Bag

## ACTIVITY SUMMARY

Participants are given sealed bags with different objects inside. By feeling the bags, participants try to identify the objects. Participants must come to a consensus about what is in each bag.

## ACTIVITY GOALS

1. To foster group communication
2. To improve group problem solving skills and cooperation with others
3. To examine the decision-making process within a group setting

## MATERIALS

1. Six small items, each in its own numbered and stapled brown bag. See directions—these can be items all from the same category, such as items found in a kitchen, or totally unrelated items.
2. Paper and pencils
3. Video camera, VCR, and TV (optional)

## DIRECTIONS

Place six items individually into stapled brown bags. These items can all be from one category, such as items found in a bathroom (a soap dish, cotton balls, toothbrush), or the items can be totally unrelated. Number each bag. The group is divided into teams of two players each. Participants must feel the stapled bag and guess, without looking, what's in the bag. Encourage members to communicate with one another and talk about their guesses. The group then writes their guesses on a piece of paper and numbers them to correspond with the numbers on the bags. When a consensus has been reached and recorded for all six bags, teams compare their guesses. Participants take turns opening the bags to verify their answers.

## VARIATIONS/TROUBLESHOOTING

1. Try this activity with two teams, three teams, or one large group. Discuss how the size of the team affects the decision-making process.

2. Try the activity both with and without providing a category for what's in the bags. Is it more difficult not having that information?

3. The facilitator can run the activity the first time and then turn it over to two or more participants to lead the second time. This "turnover" can be facilitated at the end of the first activity by asking for two volunteers to bring the items that will be placed in the bags for the next week. This game can be played several times throughout the year so that all participants will have an opportunity to lead the activity.

4. Videotape this activity and when the game is over, show the videotape. Discuss with group members what happened with the teams. Did they discuss their findings with each other or did one person take control and make all the decisions? How could they improve their strategy for the next time this game is played?

## DISCUSSION ISSUES

1. Did you talk to each other? How did you decide what was in the bag? Was it hard or easy to guess? What made it hard or easy? What did you do when you did not know the name of the item or how to spell the answer?

2. Who made the decisions in your group? Who was more passive in the decision-making process? Were there disagreements about what was in the bag? How did your group decide which guess to use? How did you decide who would write the answers down? How did the person know which answer to write down?

3. Was it easier or harder to guess if you knew the category of items? Why?

4. Describe the kinds of communication styles used by different people in the group. What kinds of communication made it easier or harder to achieve consensus? Why?

# Roadmap to Peers

## ACTIVITY SUMMARY

Participants create a village on a large sheet of poster board, agree on what items to include in their village, and then construct/draw the village together.

## ACTIVITY GOALS

1. To focus on group communication and problem solving skills
2. To focus on the importance of cooperation

## MATERIALS

1. One piece of large poster board, pens, crayons, and felt markers
2. Video camera, VCR, and TV (optional)

## DIRECTIONS

Group members sit around a poster board and are asked to design a city on the board. The facilitator can prompt group members to include homes, stores, roads, schools, and so on. For younger group members, the facilitator may ask each of them to first draw their house on the board and then, after they are finished, ask them to put in roads and important parts of the city. Be careful not to give too much help. If group members leave important aspects of a village out, they can go back and add additional items later and learn from their mistakes. When the group members have finished, discuss the items included in the village. Are there necessary services and resources such as fire and police stations, grocery stores, hospitals, and schools? Are there sufficient roads connecting all parts of the village? Did lack of communication and planning within the group lead to missing items? Encourage group members to work together and add any missing items from the city. Praise members for working together and communicating about what to add to the city.

## VARIATIONS/TROUBLESHOOTING

1. Have members work on this activity twice: one time early in the year and one time later in the year. Did communication skills improve the second time?

2. Videotape the planning and construction of the city and review the videotape with group participants. Discuss the methods used for agreeing on items put in the city. Was there agreement? Did one or two people take control or was it a group effort in planning?

3. Members with difficulties in social cognition may have a difficult time communicating what they want in the village, place structures in the village without conferring with others, or sit passively and watch the village being built. When this happens take a more active role in the activity, demonstrating the planning and problem solving skills desired.

## DISCUSSION ISSUES

1. What does each member feel is the most important part of the village?

   *My road because I can get to my friend's house.*

2. How did you decide what to add to the village?

   *Brianna and Julie took control and decided what to add.*

   What is good about the way decisions were made and what are the drawbacks?

   *It went fast because Brianna and Julie took control, but Steve did not get to have input on what went into the city.*

3. How did the planning go? What would you do differently next time?

4. What went well during the planning stage? Communicating before taking action?

# Puzzle Pieces

## ACTIVITY SUMMARY

Participants work together to reproduce an original picture as closely as possible.

## ACTIVITY GOALS

1. Encourages group communication and planning before taking action on a task
2. Helps members discuss their roles in a group planning situation such as group leader, follower, and planner

## MATERIALS

1. Photocopy the picture from the Puzzle Pieces worksheet (p. 83)
2. Paper and pencils

## DIRECTIONS

Show the group the picture from the Puzzle Pieces worksheet. Inform them that they will work as a group to make a drawing that should look exactly like the picture. The task is for each group member to draw a piece of the picture, not for one or two group members to draw the whole thing. For example, one group member will be asked to draw the vase and *only* the vase. Another group member will be asked to draw the table and only the table, and so on. Next, take each group member into a private area and assign them the piece of the picture that they will be drawing. It is preferable to tell each group member in private about the piece that they will be drawing because it encourages them to come back together and communicate with each other about the piece that they are responsible for. There are six pieces to the drawing: the table, the television, the vase, the book, the flowers, and the butterfly. If there are more than six group members have the additional group members be observers, and if there are less than six give group members more than one piece to draw. Give the group members a piece of paper and a pencil and ask them to reproduce the original drawing. Remind them that each member can only draw the piece that was assigned to them. Do not show the original drawing while they are working. The facilitator should observe how well the participants plan and execute the actual drawing. When they have finished, compare the original drawing to their picture.

## VARIATIONS/TROUBLESHOOTING

Choose a picture from a magazine that is fairly detailed. Show this picture to the group for about 5 seconds and then ask them to work together to make a drawing that is as close as possible to the original. Emphasize that if group members work together, they can come up with more details of the original than if just one person is working alone.

## DISCUSSION ISSUES

1. Do the pictures look the same?
2. How well did you plan as a group before starting to draw? Did you discuss who should draw first (e.g., should the table be drawn first and then work up from there?)? What happens if the book is drawn first? Is it hard to place the other items in relation to the book?
3. Who took the lead with this activity? Did one person direct the others?
4. What can you do differently next time to improve communication and teamwork?

# The Picnic

## ACTIVITY SUMMARY

Group members spend a few group sessions planning a picnic including where to go, permission needed, and what to take on the picnic. They then actually go on the picnic and later evaluate how well they planned it. This activity can be used a few times during the group and is especially fitting for the final group session as a group termination party.

## ACTIVITY GOALS

1. To experience the outcome of one's problem solving
2. To focus on planning and cooperation

## MATERIALS

1. Paper and pencils
2. Videotape equipment (optional)

## DIRECTIONS

Participants are asked to plan their own picnic/potluck. The group leader explains how much money they will have to spend (if it is from a classroom fund) or asks group members how much they want to spend from their own monies. The facilitator tells group members that they are responsible for bringing all items necessary for the picnic, including utensils, and then divides the group into pairs. The group as a whole decides on the category of food (e.g., drink, vegetable) that each pair will bring. Each pair then meets and discusses the particular item that they will bring in the food group assigned to them. The discussion and planning of each pair can be videotaped and viewed later. Participants are encouraged to go shopping together, make the food together, and save the receipts for all purchases. While on the picnic, group members can only use what they bring, as if they are going camping. Depending on the age of the group, it may be beneficial to take the group to a store so that they can price items and plan their purchases accordingly.

## VARIATIONS/TROUBLESHOOTING

1. Facilitators should take a very passive role in the planning stages. If mistakes are made in preparation, participants learn better if they experience the consequences of these mistakes, rather than having them corrected early on.

2. Remember that group members can only use what they bring. For example, if they forget forks and spoons, do not allow them to run down to the cafeteria or store to get some during the picnic. It is better for them to experience the real-life consequences of their planning.

## DISCUSSION ISSUES

1. How did the picnic turn out? Was everything included that was needed? Was there a good variety of food?

2. How did you decide who would bring what? How did you plan the menu? What made it successful? How would you plan better the next time?

3. How was the budget? Was there enough money? Not enough money? Did you remember your receipts?

4. If videotaped, what do you notice about the team's planning? How well did they communicate? How well did they plan? What could be done differently?

# Perspective
# Taking

P erspective taking is the ability to take and simultaneously co-ordinate a variety of perspectives. This is also known as stepping into another person's shoes. Perspective taking allows us to understand and differentiate the emotions, needs, and desires of different people in a particular situation. At the lowest levels of perspective taking, individuals may be completely egocentric and not even realize that other people even have different perspectives than their own. At the highest levels of perspective taking, individuals can step outside of a situation and examine all perspectives at the same time.

The following steps, based on the work of Robert Selman (1971; Selman & Byrne, 1974), can be used as a guide for understanding the developmental levels of perspective taking. The examples at the top are lower level skills, the bottom examples are more sophisticated behaviors. Group leaders should keep in mind that development in this area does not occur at a rapid pace. Growth in the area of perspective taking occurs over a number of years.

# Perspective Taking Steps

**1** Egocentric: Does not realize that other people have different views on a situation. Thinks that everyone has the same feelings and thoughts about a situation that he/she does. Talks mostly about self. Cannot identify the feelings of other people. Does not realize how his/her behavior affects others.

**2** Realizes that other people have different thoughts and feelings, but can't actually take the perspective of another. Can't put him/herself in another's shoes. May use the situation to help identify feelings of others. Due to difficulty with putting self into another's situation, may rely on context—e.g., he is at a birthday party so he must be happy; she got into a fight so she must be mad.

**3** Can step into another's shoes. Can understand the perspectives of others. Can look at a situation from another person's point of view. Cannot take third person perspective.

**4** Can step into another's shoes, but can also step outside of the situation and look at all perspectives at the same time. Can take the spectator perspective or third person perspective—e.g., that group started out with different views, but when Bobby gave them that last piece of information, they started thinking similarly.

# Whose View
# Is Right

## ACTIVITY SUMMARY

Group members draw, from memory, objects on a table and then compare their drawings and discuss whose drawing is the most accurate.

## ACTIVITY GOALS

1. To introduce the word and concept of perspective
2. To illustrate that people have different and unique perspectives; people see things differently

## MATERIALS

1. Paper and pencils
2. About seven different items that can be placed on a table such as a book, coffee can, chalkboard eraser, soda can, and set of keys

## DIRECTIONS

Inform group members that they will all leave the room and wait outside. While they are outside, the facilitator will place seven or so items on a table. The table should be in the middle of the room or in a place where group members can walk around the table to get a full view of the items. Instruct group members that they will come back in the room all at the same time and be given about 30 seconds to view the table. After participants view the table, ask them to go to another part of the room and without looking at the table draw a picture from memory of what the table looks like and how it is arranged.

When group members have finished, ask them to show their pictures one by one and then compare the pictures and discuss how the pictures compare with the actual table. The pictures, of course, will be different depending on where the person was standing when they looked at the table (i.e., their view or perspective) and their memory. Begin a discussion with group members of the reasons for the pictures being different. The pictures "should be" the same because they all looked at the same table. Emphasize that even though all looked at the same situation, everyone had a different view or perspective. No one is "right." In order to get an accurate picture of how the table was arranged, all perspectives must be considered.

## DISCUSSION ISSUES

1. Why does everyone have a different picture? You all looked at the same thing!

2. What were items that some people missed? Was it because those people were standing where they could not see the item? It is important to get different perspectives on the same situation.

# Walking Game

## ACTIVITY SUMMARY

One person stands in front of the group and depicts an emotion through walking. Others must guess how the person feels and make guesses about why she/he feels that way.

## ACTIVITY GOALS

1. To focus on the meaning of nonverbal body language

2. To increase emotional vocabulary

3. To help identify the feelings of others

## MATERIALS

1. Video camera, VCR, and TV (optional)

## DIRECTIONS

Tell the group that this activity focuses on nonverbal body language. The facilitator may want to initiate a short discussion on the meaning of nonverbal body language (i.e., communication without words). One person is then chosen to go first and this person is told to walk in a way that depicts an emotion. The facilitator may give examples to help the group get started. For example, "Walk like someone is following you" (nervous) or "You are walking to your birthday party" (excited). Other group members are told not only to guess the emotion, but also to try and guess the context of the walk. Points are given to participants for correct answers.

## VARIATIONS/TROUBLESHOOTING

1. Divide the group into teams. Each team invents a team name (asking the team to choose a name encourages group

problem solving and cooperation) and teams compete against each other during the activity.

2. Some individuals, especially younger group members or less advanced groups, may have a difficult time thinking of a feeling word on their own or developing the context of the emotion. Have ready a stack of index cards with a feeling word and scenario for that feeling written on each. Group members will choose a card to act out. Examples include (a) walk as if you are creeping past a sleeping German shepherd and are scared, (b) walk as if you are feeling nervous (or loving) and trying not to wake a sleeping baby, (c) walk as if you are scared and are trying to get home before the thunderstorm hits, (d) walk as if you are depressed because of a bad grade on a test, and (e) walk as if you are hopeful that there will be homemade pie at home.

3. Videotape each member's depiction of the emotion and show the videotape when the game is over. Discuss how the emotion could have been depicted differently.

## DISCUSSION ISSUES

1. How does your body show how you feel?

   *You move faster when you are scared, slower when you're bored or reluctant. When nervous, your eyes become watchful.*

2. What could be done to make the scenario clearer?

3. What did the person do that helped you guess?

# Hide and Seek

## ACTIVITY SUMMARY

The group is divided into teams of two. One team member guides his/her teammate to a hidden object using clues such as cold, warm, and hot.

## ACTIVITY GOAL

1. To learn how to adjust communication, specifically directions, to meet the needs of another
2. To develop listening skills and following directions

## MATERIALS

1. An object to hide such as hard candy or erasers. A bag of hard candy is good because participants can eat the candy when done

## DIRECTIONS

The facilitator asks for a volunteer to find an object that the facilitator will hide. The facilitator shows the volunteer two pieces of candy that will be hidden and informs her/him that if she/he finds them, then both the facilitator and the volunteer will get to keep one piece of candy. The facilitator asks the volunteer to leave the room and the facilitator hides the candy in the room (hide the candy so it is difficult to find). Ask the volunteer to return and start looking for the candy. As the person is searching, talk with the group about how difficult the activity is. The volunteer has no idea where to start looking; the candy can be anywhere! Ask group members if there is anything that can be done to make the activity easier. Guide group members into a discussion of giving clues such as "hot" for close and "cold " for far away. Use the clues, including increments of these (e.g., icy, very warm, burning hot), to help guide the volunteer to the object. Next, divide the group into teams of two and have them take turns hiding and finding the candy using the hot and cold clues. Other teams that are not participating should watch the current team play and learn techniques to make the game easier.

## DISCUSSION ISSUES

1. What was most helpful thing the person giving directions did? Did the person giving directions pay attention to the seeker and give more frequent clues when needed?

2. What helpful strategy did the person looking for the candy use?

# Guess the Feeling

## ACTIVITY SUMMARY

One group member stands in front of the group and depicts a single feeling/emotion using body language. Other members try to guess what emotion is being depicted. Points are given for correct answers.

## ACTIVITY GOALS

1. To examine how body language shows how one feels
2. To develop emotional vocabulary

## MATERIALS

1. Feeling words printed on index cards: for younger and less advanced groups, choose five basic feeling words such as happy, sad, mad, scared, and surprised; for more advanced groups, choose 10 or more feeling words from the list on pages 98–99.

## DIRECTIONS

Prior to the group, the group facilitator must determine the group members' knowledge of emotional vocabulary. For some groups, the facilitator may want to choose 5 feeling words with which to play. For advanced groups, the facilitator may want a longer list of feeling words, up to 15 or more. The facilitator first presents the index cards with printed feeling words, one by one. Group members are asked to give the meaning of the word. When each feeling word has been reviewed, the game begins. One person elects to go first and chooses a feeling word from the stack of index cards. She/he then acts out the word using facial expression and body language. Whoever guesses correctly from the group wins one point and is the next person to act out a word. The game continues until the agreed-upon stop point (for example, the first person to acquire 10 points).

## VARIATIONS/TROUBLESHOOTING

1. Facilitators should avoid a laborious period of teaching (such as giving the correct spelling of feeling words).
2. This activity can be played many times during the group period, each time adding new feeling words.
3. This activity can be varied to resemble charades. In this variation, the group is divided into two teams. One member acts out a feeling word for his/her team and the team gets a point for guessing the correct feeling.

## DISCUSSION ISSUES

1. Why was one presentation easier to guess than another?

   *Jorge's was hard to guess because he just stood there with an expression on his face but with no body language.*

2. How do you learn how other people are feeling? For example, how do you know how people in your family feel?

# Feeling Words

abandoned

afraid

aggravated

aggressive

alarmed

amused

angry

annoyed

anxious

appreciated

blue

bored

burned up

calm

carefree

cautious

cheerful

concerned

confident

confused

content

crushed

curious

defeated

dejected

delighted

depressed

desperate

disgusted

drained

embarrassed

empty

enthusiastic

excited

flexible

focused

frightened

frustrated

glad

gloomy

glum

grief-stricken

guilty

happy

hateful

helpless

hopeless

horrified

hostile

hurt

inadequate

independent

insecure

irritated

joyous

lonely

mad

miserable

nervous

outraged

overwhelmed

panicked

peaceful

pleased

powerful

pressured

proud

relieved

sad

satisfied

scared

shameful

shocked

shy

stuck

surprised

sympathetic

tense

terrified

uneasy

unsure

violated

vulnerable

worried

worthless

# Feeling Skits

## ACTIVITY SUMMARY

The group is divided into teams and each team acts out a feeling word using a skit. The other team tries to guess the feeling being depicted.

## ACTIVITY GOALS

1. To focus on group planning and communication
2. To develop role-taking skills

## MATERIALS

1. Depending on the group, the facilitator may wish to review a list of feeling words using index cards with feelings words printed on them. (See pages 98–99 for a list of suggested words.)

## DIRECTIONS

Divide the group into workable teams (usually two to three members) with at least three teams competing. Ask teams to choose three feeling words and develop three different skits that depict the three feeling words. Teams usually require about 10 minutes to prepare and, if possible, should be encouraged to practice in private before playing the game. Teams then take turns presenting their skits. After each skit, the other teams compete to see who can guess the feeling word being acted out. One point is given to the team that correctly guesses the feeling word and to the team presenting the skit. If, after a certain number of guesses, the correct answer is not given, no team gets a point and the next skit is presented.

## VARIATIONS/TROUBLESHOOTING

1. Encourage group members to discuss with their team mem-

bers before guessing. If one member impulsively guesses without discussing with team members and the answer is wrong, then this is counted as a wrong answer. This way, individuals will experience the natural consequences of impulsive guessing.

2. The facilitator may wish to ask the members of the guessing team to write down their guesses individually and win points individually. This helps ensure full participation and it helps the facilitator evaluate individual progress in the group.

## DISCUSSION ISSUES

1. How did you arrive at that guess? What was the giveaway or best clue? How did body language help you guess?

2. Was one skit easier to guess than another? Why?

# And I Felt...

## ACTIVITY SUMMARY

Participants take turns telling about an incident in their lives. At the end of each story, other group members identify the story-teller's feelings. Points are given for correct guesses.

## ACTIVITY GOALS

1. To better connect a person's experience and her/his feelings
2. To increase emotional vocabulary

## MATERIALS

1. Paper and pencils

## DIRECTIONS

Ask each person to think of an incident in his/her life that he/she wants to talk about, think of how he/she felt during that incident, and write the feeling word down. Each person then takes turns telling his/her story, but omitting how he/she felt during the incident. At the end of each story, participants should say" . . . and I felt_____." Other students then write down how they think the person felt. Points are given for correct answers (example: "I was at school paying attention to the teacher when I felt a jolt. I wasn't sure what was going on until I felt the second jolt and the floor started moving in a wave-like fashion. Realizing that it was an earthquake, I quickly slid under the table and I felt_____!"). Write down a brief summary of the story and the feeling word on each participant's personal poster.

## VARIATIONS/TROUBLESHOOTING

1. Instead of telling about the incident, members can act out the incident.

2. For younger and less advanced group members, ask members to draw a picture of when they felt a certain emotion. For example, ask all participants to draw a picture of when they felt happy in the past (or what made them happy in the past) and give examples that they can use such as a surprise birthday party, going to the amusement park, or going swimming. When all have finished, one by one have them show their pictures and have others guess what the picture is about and what made that person happy. Repeat this game with different feeling words (e.g., What made you feel mad in the past? What made you feel sad scared in the past?).

## DISCUSSION ISSUES

1. How did you guess what their feeling was? What was the clue?
2. Why was one story easier to guess than another?
3. How do we learn how other people are feeling when they do not tell us?

# Soap Opera

## ACTIVITY SUMMARY

Members watch segments of a soap opera without the use of sound/caption and make guesses about how the characters are feeling and what could be going on in that particular scene.

## ACTIVITY GOALS

1. To focus on understanding the perspective of others
2. To practice reading of social situations using behavioral cues and facial expressions
3. To increase emotional vocabulary

## MATERIALS

1. Copy a segment of a soap opera. Soap operas were chosen because the characters are often dramatic and the story line is lively. Your soap opera segment should be between 30 seconds and 1 minute, should focus on one or two characters, and of course be age-appropriate for the group. If possible, they should be copied with captions for full accessibility.
2. VCR and TV

## DIRECTIONS

The group facilitator shows a soap opera segment to the group without sound or caption. Group members write down what they think the characters felt and what was going on in the scene. The segment is then replayed with sound (interpreted) or captions, and members discuss who was the closest to being correct. Another segment is then shown and the group continues in the same manner.

# DISCUSSION ISSUES

1. Was it easy or hard to guess how characters were feeling? Why/why not?

2. How did you guess what they were feeling (facial expression, body movement)?

3. How did you guess at the story line? Were you right?

4. What gave you clues about the story?

# Who Is It

## ACTIVITY SUMMARY

One member portrays another person and the group members guess who that person is.

## ACTIVITY GOALS

1. To focus on perspective taking through role play

2. To practice putting oneself in another's shoes

## MATERIALS

None

## DIRECTIONS

Ask group members to think of a person that all of the group members know of, such as the school principal, the U.S. president, a well-known teacher, or a famous movie or rock star. Some group members will probably be able to choose a person without help from the facilitator. Others may have difficulty choosing someone appropriate for this activity and will need guidance from the facilitator. Each group member will then take turns role playing this person and the group member that correctly guesses the identity of the person being depicted wins a point.

## VARIATIONS/TROUBLESHOOTING

To make the game more challenging, after each group member thinks of someone to depict ask him/her to make a list of the physical characteristics, emotions, and personality characteristics that he/she plans to depict. Other group members then get points not only for guessing the identity of the person, but also for guessing the physical characteristics, emotions, and personality characteristics being shown; a point can be given for each characteristic correctly guessed.

## DISCUSSION ISSUES

1. What unique characteristics does the person that you chose to depict have? What characteristics were easy to act out? Difficult to act out?

2. For the group members guessing, was it easy or hard to guess the identity? Why?

3. List the different physical, emotional, and personality characteristics being depicted.

# This Really Happened

## ACTIVITY SUMMARY

Participants act out an incident from their team member's life and others guess what happened during the incident and how the person involved felt.

## ACTIVITY GOALS

1. To practice putting oneself in another's shoes
2. To focus on communication skills

## MATERIALS

None

## DIRECTIONS

Group members are divided into pairs and each person is asked to think of a recent incident and how they felt during that incident. The facilitator can give examples, such as dropping one's tray at lunch, arriving at your own surprise party, getting a good grade on a test, and so on. Team members take turns telling his/her story to his/her partner including the feeling(s) experienced. The teams then come back together as a larger group and each person role plays his/her partner's incident. Other teams win points for (1) describing what happened and (2) what the person involved felt. Write down what happened to each person on his/her personal poster.

## DISCUSSION ISSUES

1. Did your team member accurately depict what happened to you?

2. Was it easier to guess what happened during the incident or how the person felt? Why?

3. Would other members have felt the same way if that incident happened to them?

*Jeffrey learns his cat is lost and is very scared. Nadine knows if her cat is missing she is probably in the neighborhood. Nadine would not be scared or worried.*

# What's In Your Future

## ACTIVITY SUMMARY

Participants role play what they think others will be doing in the future.

## ACTIVITY GOAL

1. To better infer the future job or activity of others using what is known about that person

## MATERIALS

1. Paper and pencils
2. Container for small papers

## DIRECTIONS

Each member writes his/her name on a piece of paper and puts the paper in a container. Each person draws a name without showing the others. Members should think about this person's personality and guess what this person will be doing in the future. They can focus on jobs or leisure time activities, but the choice of the future activity must be supported by present or past behaviors/personality characteristics of the person. Each participant then tells which name they picked and acts out what she/he thinks this person will be doing in the future. Other members try to guess the future activity. Write this information on each person's personal poster. Points are given for correct answers.

## VARIATIONS/TROUBLESHOOTING

1. Adjust the level of difficulty by asking members not to tell

the name that they have chosen and others must guess the name and the activity.

## DISCUSSION ISSUES

1. Do you think that she/he might be correct in predicting your future? Why or why not? If not, act out what you will be doing in the future.

2. How did you choose that particular job for that person?

   *She/he likes sports so I thought that she/he would become a sportscaster.*

# Handling Difficult
# Group Issues

Groups will not always run as expected or hoped. This is especially true when conducting activities with individuals who have difficulties in social functioning. This section provides some practical suggestions to address common group problems that might emerge during groups.

# Common Situations and Suggestions

### 1. Facilitator is unsure about which activities are appropriate for the group's skill level.

Use a trial-and-error method. If one activity seems too easy for group members, make the activity harder by using a recommendation in the variations section or move on to a more difficult activity. Facilitators may also be unsure about which category of learning (person conceptualization, perspective taking, problem solving, or communication) to target. This is to be expected, especially during the first meetings of the group. With some groups, after a few months, a pattern emerges, such as one of the four categories presents noticeable difficulties. If so, this category can be targeted. If not, continue with the activities that seem most interesting for the group members.

### 2. Group members complain that they are bored.

Often boredom is caused by an activity being too difficult for the group and can be resolved by initiating an easier activity. However, if degree of difficulty is not the issue, the facilitator may encourage group problem solving. Ask members what would make the group more fun. List their ideas on the board. It is important to give the group control in following through with their suggestions. The facilitator can discuss with the group which suggestions are appropriate and possible (such as bringing food to the group) and which suggestions are inappropriate or not possible. Another approach is to have two or three participants prepare and lead a group session.

### 3. One member does not want to participate.

Use this opportunity to have the group learn more about this person (person conceptualization). This situation can be developed into a perspective-taking game. Ask other group members to guess what they think this person would rather be doing. Then the nonparticipating person can judge whether the guesses are correct or incorrect. Ask others to guess what it would take for this person to participate. Give points for correct answers (e.g., $1,000,000, a trip to Disneyland, a new car). Maybe this person would like to help direct the activity. What is this person comfortable doing? Maybe this person would like to keep score during the game. The point is not to force the person to participate with threats of punishment, but to learn more about him/her.

### 4. The group goes off topic.

Sometimes groups will go off topic and discuss other issues. These issues may be more important to the group members at that time. It may be helpful to use these group-initiated topics in an activity. For example, when the World Trade Center was attacked on September 11, 2001, one group wrote down how they felt on a piece of paper and put these papers into a container. They then took turns choosing a piece of paper and guessing who felt which way. Discussion of feelings happened throughout the game.

### 5. A very serious topic emerges in the group.

These group is not designed to be a therapy group. If a group member initiates a topic of a serious nature, the facilitator should steer the group back to a more general discussion and follow up with the individual later and make the appropriate referrals.

### 6. Group members seem to have a difficult time understanding the game.

When group members have a difficult time understanding a game, they can become easily distracted. They may lose motivation to participate. If this happens, simplify the activity. For example, instead of using 15 feeling words for "Guess the Feeling," use 5. Instead of using 10 pictures for "Lunch Date," use 3. In addition, decrease the amount of verbal directions. Try starting the activity with very few directions and explain as you go along. Or, if some of the group members understand an activity, go ahead and start playing the game. By observing, the others can join as soon as they understand the rules of the game.

**7. A conflict arises among group members.**

Conflicts which happen in school or in group situations are good opportunities to use practice problem solving skills. When a conflict occurs, role play can be used to focus on the conflict in order to begin problem solving. The facilitator asks for volunteers to role play the conflict. Sometimes it is best for the people directly involved with the conflict to act as "role-play directors" instead of as actors. This helps diffuse some of the intense feelings that people who were directly involved in the conflict may have. The role play is then conducted while the role-play directors guide the role play to ensure accuracy. After the role play, observers and actors are asked to write down the feelings of the people involved in the conflict and the role-play directors are asked to write down how they actually felt during the situation. Group members then compare what they wrote down with how the involved people actually felt. Group members can also write down and discuss how the problem could be handled differently. This problem solving method is very flexible. Facilitators can adjust the directions depending on what is appropriate for their particular group.

# References
# and Suggestions
# for Further Reading

---

## DEAFNESS AND PSYCHOSOCIAL DEVELOPMENT

Greenberg, M.T., & Kusche, C. A. (1993). *Promoting the Social and Emotional Development in Deaf Children: The PATHS Project*. Seattle, WA: University of Washington Press.

Describes the PATHS (Promoting Alternative Thinking Strategies) curriculum, a program to facilitate the social and emotional development in elementary-school-age children. It includes a thorough review of research on the social–emotional development of deaf children.

Heiling, K., (1995). *The Development of Deaf Children: Academic Achievement Levels and Social Processes* (translated by Gunilla Layer). Signum: Germany.

Covers the research on social development of deaf children, including factors that positively influence language and social development.

## MEDIATED INTERVENTION

Feuerstein, R. (1980). *Instructional Enrichment: An Intervention Program for Cognitive Modifiability.* Baltimore, MD: University Park Press.

See also web site: www.icelp.org for the International Center for the Enhancement of Learning Potential. Describes Feuerstein's theory of mediated intervention and research. Web site contains reading material and training opportunities related to the role of mediator in education.

## PERSON CONCEPTUALIZATION

Peevers, B. H., & Secord, P. F. (1973). Developmental changes in attribution of descriptive concepts of person. *Journal of Personality and Social Psychology, 27,* 120–128.

Describes person perception and developmental levels.

Livesley, W. J., & Bromley, D. B. (1973). *Person Perception in Childhood and Adolescence.* London: Wiley.
Overview of person conceptualization and relevant research.

## PERSPECTIVE TAKING

Selman, R. L. (1971). Taking another's perspective: Role-taking development in early childhood. *Child Development, 42,* 1721–1734.

Selman, R. L., & Byrne, D. F. (1974). A structural–developmental analysis of role-taking in middle childhood. *Child Development, 45,* 803-806.

# ABOUT THE AUTHORS

Mimi W. Lou, Ph.D., worked at the University of California Center on Deafness (UCCD) from 1980 to 1993. Lou is currenlty the clinical director of the Children's Hospital Autism Intervention program in Oakland, CA.

Elizabeth Stone Charlson, Ph.D., worked at UCCD from 1991 to 1996. Charlson is currently a member of the faculty at San Francisco State University in the Department of Child and Adolescent Development.

Stephen M. Gage, M.S., L.P.C., worked at UCCD from 1991 to 1995. Gage has a private practice as a Mental Health Therapist and is a Clinical Fellow with the Child Development/Community Policing Program in Charlotte, NC.

Nancy Moser, L.C.S.W., is the Executive Director at UCCD. Moser is also a clinical consultant for the California State School for the Deaf in Fremont, and an instructor at San Francisco State University.